D1100039

THE
BLITZED
BRITS

TERRY DEARY

Inside illustrations by Kate Sheppard

Brought to you by

The Daily Telegraph

This book is for the staff
of the Durham Light Infantry Museum
in Durham City, with thanks

This edition is produced for The Daily Telegraph

Scholastic Children's Books, Euston House, 24 Eversholt Street, London, NW1 1DB

For promotional use only. Not for resale

Selling or purchasing this book on the internet or otherwise may constitute a criminal offence.

First published in the UK by Scholastic Ltd, 1994

ISBN 1 4071 0277 X

Typeset by Rapid Reprographics
Printed and bound by Nørhaven Paperback A/S, Denmark

CONTENTS

Horrible Histories:
The Savage Stone Age
The Awesome Egyptians
The Groovy Greeks
The Rotten Romans
The Cut-throat Celts
The Smashing Saxons
The Vicious Vikings
The Stormin' Normans
The Measly Middle Ages
The Angry Aztecs
The Incredible Incas
The Terrible Tudors
Even More Terrible Tudors
The Slimy Stuarts
The Gorgeous Georgians
The Vile Victorians
The Barmy British Empire
The Frightful First World War
The Woeful Second World War
The Blitzed Brits

Horrible Histories Specials:
Bloody Scotland
Cruel Kings and Mean Queens
Dark Knights and Dingy Castles
France
Ireland
Rowdy Revolutions
The 20th Century
The USA
Wicked Words

Also available:
The Awesome Ancient Quiz Book
Dreadful Diary
Horrible Christmas
The Horribly Huge Quiz Book
Loathsome Letter-writing Pack
The Mad Millennium Play

INTRODUCTION

Once upon a time history lessons were all about things that happened hundreds of years ago. If you weren't dead then you weren't history. And it's pretty hard to be lively about dead people. History was BORING.

Then, in the 1980s, teachers suddenly realised that **yesterday** is History . . . and last week is practically ancient history! Parents are as interesting as Julius Caesar. History lessons changed . . . you couldn't interview Julius Caesar, but you could interview parents . . .

Of course grandparents have even older memories.

Still, they were pretty young at the time. They may have known **what** happened, but they didn't understand exactly **why** it happened as it did.

And teachers can't answer such vital questions because **their** teachers never told them the answers.

So, what you need is a history book that tells you the answers to the **really** important questions. How did people live? And **why** did they live like that? Then you can understand your history . . . **and** your grandparents! What you need is a book called *Horrible Histories – The Blitzed Brits*.

And, by a strange chance, you just happen to have started reading it! So carry on . . .

BLITZED BRIT TIMELINE

27 January 1923 First meeting of the Nazi party in Germany. Leader, Adolf Hitler.

15 March 1933 Adolf Hitler and his Nazis take power in Germany. They rule by terror.

3 January 1938 Nervous British Government fears Nazi invasion and promises to give a gas mask to every British schoolchild.

31 March 1939 British Prime Minister, Neville Chamberlain, makes a promise to Poland . . . *If Germany invades you then Britain and France will help.*

1 September 1939 Germany invades Poland. The British Government, afraid of war, orders women and children in the cities to be 'evacuated' into the safe countryside.

3 September 1939 Britain declares war on Germany – World War Two begins. The air-raid sirens sound for the first time. People rush around like headless chickens looking for shelter – but it's a false alarm.

8 January 1940 It's the coldest winter for half a century. The Thames freezes. Ships bringing food to Britain are being sunk by German submarines. The Government fears a food shortage . . . so the first foods go on ration.

1 February 1940 A 'blackout' is ordered. No lights to be shown at night so enemy bombers can't see where to drop their bombs. Deaths on the blacked-out roads have doubled! Speed limit of 20 m.p.h. for cars at night.

10 May 1940 Germany attacks Holland and Belgium. Their armies march towards France – and the English Channel . . . Britain next? Winston Churchill is elected Prime Minister.

14 May 1940 Men aged 17 to 65 invited to join the Local Defence Volunteers – a million join. Later known as the Home Guard – **better** known as *Dad's Army*.

30 May 1940 The beaten British Army comes home from Dunkirk – they're picked up on the French beaches by hundreds of little boats from England.

WE'LL SHOW 'EM

31 May 1940 A new law says:

All signposts have to be removed.

Church bells can only be rung as a sign of invasion.

All foreigners in the country must be locked up or made to report to the police.

18 June 1940 Winston Churchill tells the people that the battle in France is lost . . . *I expect that the Battle of Britain is about to begin. The whole fury and might of the enemy must soon be turned on us.*

10 July 1940 First of the large air raids. This is the real start of the Battle of Britain in the skies. Lady Reading (head of Women's Voluntary Service) appeals to families to give up their aluminium pots and pans to make aeroplanes. *We can all have the thrill of thinking, when we hear the*

THIS'LL NEVER GET OFF THE GROUND

9

news of a battle in the air, 'Perhaps it was my saucepan that made a part of that Hurricane plane.'

16 July 1940 Hitler signs order for Operation Sealion – the invasion of England. Order 2a is the problem. 'The RAF must be eliminated.' Easier said than done! Sealion never happens.

13 August 1940 All-out German air raids lasting two days. Britain **says** that 185 enemy aircraft were shot down. (The true number was 60.)

24 August 1940 The Germans bomb London by mistake after Hitler had told them not to! So the British bomb Berlin in revenge . . . so the Germans bomb London . . . and so it goes on.

7 September 1940 Code word 'Cromwell' passed to home defence forces. This meant, 'Be on your guard – it's a good night for an invasion'. But some officers thought it meant, 'The invasion has started'! They blew up bridges – and themselves – and generally panicked everyone.

7 September 1940 Germany is losing too many bombers in daylight raids. They switch to night raids. This is the real start of the blitz.

14 November 1940 Air raids switch to Coventry for a while. This is where a lot of British war machinery is being made. Next morning nearly everyone claimed to know someone who'd been killed or injured in the city.

10 May 1941 Heaviest – and last – big bombing raid on London until 1944. House of Commons wrecked. Hitler 1 – Guy Fawkes 0.

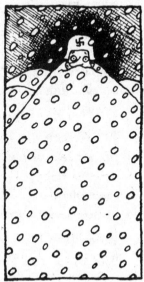

1 June 1941 Clothing is rationed – but not **only** because clothes are in short supply! It was also to set clothing workers free to work in war factories.

22 June 1941 Germany invades Russia. This was a big mistake and probably lost them the War. Hitler could beat the Russian Army – he couldn't beat the Russian winter. Snow 1 – Hitler 0.

11

September 1941 The Government orders that most iron railings should be taken down and the metal used for the war effort – Buckingham Palace included.

December 1941 Japanese aircraft sink American ships in the Pacific Ocean so United States of America joins the war on Britain's side – at last.

February 1942 It's illegal to decorate cups, saucers and plates for sale – it's a waste of precious manufacturing time that could be spent making war items.

February 1942 Soap is put on ration – one small bar of soap had to last you four weeks. (Some scruffy kids could make it last a year!)

13 March 1942 The end of private motoring – only essential users will be allowed petrol. But, remember, only one family in ten owned a car anyway.

June 1942 It's illegal to make bedspreads and table-cloths.

2 February 1943 German soldiers

surrender in Stalingrad (Russia). The War is turning against them.

8 September 1943 Now Italy declares war on their old ally, Germany!

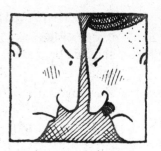

December 1943 Eighteen-year-old boys who don't join the army are made to work in coal mines. Mr Ernest Bevin thought up this law, so the young miners became known as Bevin Boys.

6 June 1944 Britain and her allies invade Europe.

16 June 1944 The first Flying Bombs land on London. A new blitz is beginning. People nickname the V1 (Vee One) rockets 'Doodlebugs' and 'Buzz bombs'. But V1 really stands for 'Revenge Weapon 1'.

8 September 1944 The first V2 rockets arrive. Quieter and more destructive than the V1s . . . but the Government doesn't admit there are such things until 10 November!

14 November 1944 Home Guard abolished. The danger of invasion has passed.

13

24 April 1945 End of blackout except on coast.

6 May 1945 Germany surrenders – end of war in Europe.

8 May 1945 Victory in Europe (V.E. Day) – holiday and parties.

6 August 1945 The United States drops the first atomic bomb on Japan – Japan surrenders shortly after. End of World War Two.

Things they shouldn't have said

Neville Chamberlain, British Prime Minister, in 1938 after signing a peace treaty with Germany

R.H. Naylor,
astrologer in the Sunday Express

14

BEAT THE BLITZ

Could you have survived an air raid? Answer these questions to see what your chances would be . . .

1 The air-raid sirens sound. Planes appear overhead. You are a long way from an air raid shelter. As bombs fall do you . . .

a run for home (shouting 'I want my Mam!')

b stand still (and cross your fingers)

c lie down where you are

2 An incendiary bomb lands near your house. This sort of bomb doesn't explode. It just burns fiercely. As the fire spreads towards your house, do you . . .

a pour a bucket of water over it

b go to your nearest shelter and let it burn

c shovel sand or soil over it

3 A bomb lands in your back garden. It sinks into the soil but does not explode – yet. Do you . . .

a throw stones at it so it will go off and not catch some unsuspecting passer-by

b tiptoe to your nearest shelter – any shelter except the one in the garden!

c tell your local ARP Warden

4 As a raid starts you head for the Anderson Shelter in your garden. It is half underground and has a thick cushion of soil over the roof. You should be safer here than in the house. But you realise that the family cat is missing. Do you . . .
a go out and look for it and stay out until you find it
b stay in the shelter but leave the shelter door open so the cat can find its own way in
c shut the shelter door

5 Do you take your gas mask with you . . .
a whenever you hear the air-raid warnings sound
b whenever you go out and have a spare hand to carry it
c always
6 An ARP warden walks down the street spinning a rattle of the sort that football supporters used to use. You don't know what this means. Do you . . .
a shout 'Up United!' and follow him to see if there's a game on
b ask someone what it means
c put your gas mask on
7 You wake up to the sound of bombs exploding. A raid is happening and there's been no warning! In the

blackout you can see explosions coming closer and closer. Do you . . .

a watch to see where the next bomb will land

b get dressed and head for the nearest shelter

c grab your gas mask and hide under your bed

8 You want to make your shelter more comfortable. Do you . . .

a take an electric cable from the house so you can have electric light and an electric fire

b fit a wooden door to keep the draught out

c take a candle for light and a blanket to put across the door for draughts

9 You have no shelter at home. Do you . . .

a shelter upstairs in your bedroom

b go to a public shelter

c turn a downstairs room into a bedroom and shelter there

Answers: Mostly **a** – the bad news is that you'd probably be too dead to read this. Maybe you have a death wish, maybe you haven't listened to the Government advice, maybe you panic easily . . . or maybe you're just a bit dim.

Anyway, if you are an **a** person you probably wouldn't survive the blitz unless you were very, very lucky. It wouldn't be wise to run around the streets in a blackout, to treat bombs like big fireworks or to stand near a window during a raid – a nearby blast might not knock your house down but the flying glass would shred you!

Mostly **b** - like many people in the War you knew what you were supposed to do but sometimes got a bit careless or forgetful. If you were lucky you could make a **b** mistake and get away with it. On the other hand it could be the last mistake you ever made! The only good news is that you're not as thick as the people who answer **a**.

Mostly **c** – you've followed all the Government advice. This gives you the best chance of surviving. Of course, it's easy to read this and think how clever you are. It's different actually being caught in an air raid. Even people who knew the advice could panic and make a mistake that cost them their lives.

Blitzed bomb shelters

Before the War there was a really rotten report on air raids. The Air Ministry reckoned there would be . . .

700 tons of bombs dropped on British cities **every day**
600,000 deaths a year

So they . . .

- printed a million burial forms – just to be on the safe side

THAT SHOULD DO IT.

- started to stockpile hundreds of cardboard coffins
  No wonder the British people were worried!

(The Air Ministry was wrong! In fact 300,000 died during the six years of the war . . . more than half of them in London.)

The Ministry of Home Security took charge of Air Raid Precautions (ARP) and announced:

EVERYONE WHO HAS NO FORM OF SHELTER SHOULD BUSY HIMSELF AT ONCE WITH SELECTING AND PREPARING A REFUGE ROOM

Ministry of Home Security leaflet 3 September 1940

The Government wouldn't build your shelter. The local council dumped the bits at your door and left you to get on with it.

Bomb shelter fact file

1 The Government banned people from sheltering in the London Underground train stations during an air raid. But they couldn't stop people buying a half-pence platform ticket and refusing to come up! In the end the Government dropped the ban.

2 By the end of September almost 200,000 people were using the Underground for shelter every night. They were fitted out with bunk beds and a library service was provided.

3 Some stations had closed off their toilets. If you wanted to use the toilet then you probably had to take a train to the next station. Soon 'bucket' toilets were provided. Yeuch!

4 Christmas 1940 saw the Underground stations decorated with streamers, and Christmas parties were held during the air raids.

5 If you wanted to stay in your home during the bombing then you could have a Morrison shelter. It was like a steel table with wire-mesh sides and a mattress underneath. Two adults and two small children could squeeze under – but one very fat person could get stuck!

6 In an air raid, any shelter was better than none. In a town in south-west England a young mother was caught in the street with her baby. She quickly popped the baby into a dustbin.

7 One father said, 'We don't need a shelter. Those Anderson shelters are just corrugated iron. They're no more than garden sheds. Our house is stronger.' Then he saw a house that had been  flattened by a bomb. The Anderson shelter next to it had survived. He bought one the same day!

8 In Middlesbrough a popular verse gave a bit of advice:

IN A RAID, IF YOU MUST LOSE YOUR HEAD
REMEMBER THE THINGS THAT YOU HAVE READ
YOU'LL KNOW WHAT TO DO
FOR THERE'LL ONLY BE TWO
KINDS OF PEOPLE
THE QUICK AND THE DEAD

9 One of the nastiest facts about the air raids was that your house was unguarded while you went into a shelter. If your house was damaged then it could well be 'looted' – anything worthwhile was stolen. And not just by professional burglars. Neighbours might grab something of yours – so did the Air Raid Precaution Wardens, the demolition men – even the police! One family left their home when an unexploded bomb landed in their potato patch – the bomb was removed and the family returned . . . but there wasn't a single potato to be found!

10 Even a bombed house played its part in the war effort! The rubble was carted off to the countryside to build new runways for the Royal Air Force.

Did you know?
Sand bags were kept at the foot of lamp posts in towns. If there was a fire-bomb then you knew where to look for sand to smother it with. Good idea? Well . . . dogs use lamp posts as toilets. They loved the sand bags! So when you grabbed a sand bag it was always stinking and

usually mouldy – and the smelly sand often fell out of the bottom!

Barrage balloons

The blitzed Brits were especially afraid of dive-bombers. These aeroplanes swooped low to drop their bombs. To stop this sort of bombing, barrage balloons were invented.

These were huge, silvery balloons, each as big as a house. They were filled with gas and floated over towns, held down by heavy steel cables. Dive-bombers were torn apart by these cables.

Many people felt safe under the cover of these silver cigar-shaped balloons. One boy described them as 'herds of silver elephants' as they rose, glittering in the sun. But they also caused some problems . . .

Five fearful facts about barrage balloons

1 Sometimes the cables on a balloon snapped and the balloon floated away. They made good target practice for fighter planes.

2 Have you ever blown up a party balloon and let go of the end? If a barrage balloon got a split in it then it would charge round the sky in a similar way.

3 A balloon could catch fire – from a lightning strike or an enemy aeroplane attack. Then it could start to come down on the town below. It could be as deadly as a bomb landing on your roof!

4 A loose balloon trailed its wires. If they caught overhead power cables they could leave a town without power for several hours.

5 A trailing cable caught a Women's Royal Air Force worker (WRAF) on the back of the head. She cried with the pain and held her head in her hands. It was just as well she did . . . when she got to hospital her neck was found to be broken. If she hadn't held her head straight she would have died.

A blitzed ghost story

Thousands of people died in the blitz. It's not surprising that many people have stories about death and stories of the supernatural . . .

Megan Davies woke up suddenly. It was a nightmare that had shaken her from a peaceful sleep. She struggled to remember it. The details were faint, but the young woman knew it was something to do with her mother. There was danger in that dream. Perhaps even death.

It was still dark in the Welsh village cottage. Megan struck a match and lit the oil lamp. She dressed quickly and hurried down to breakfast.

'Penny for your thoughts,' her mother said as the young woman chewed slowly on her toast.

'What was that?'

'I said, what are you thinking about? You look worried.'

Megan looked away. 'Nothing, Mam.'

'There's something on your mind. What is it?'

Megan didn't want to tell her mother about the dream. 'I've got to get to work, Mam.'

'I want to know what's wrong – a problem shared is a problem halved.'

'I'll tell you when I get home tonight, Mam,' Megan promised. She grabbed her hat and ran for the bus.

She worked as well as she could. But the gloom of the dream dampened her day. As the bus climbed the valley towards her home that evening she prayed softly to herself. She prayed that she'd never have to tell her mother about that dream.

And, when she reached home, it seemed as if her prayer had been answered. Her mother was more worried about Megan being late than about her daughter's morning mood. 'Got a rabbit from the butcher. Nearly gone dry in the oven it has!'

'Sorry, Mam!'

'Pat's eaten hers.'

Megan smiled at the young evacuee girl. 'Rabbit pie and a safe house. You're a lucky girl.'

Pat looked back with a slight frown. 'No bomb shelter,' was all she said.

Megan sighed. 'You don't need bomb shelters in the country, Pat. Don't worry . . . Mr Hitler isn't going to waste his bombs on our little village.'

Pat didn't look too sure.

And it was Pat who ran down the stairs later that night crying, 'German bomber! German bomber!'

'Just a bad dream,' Mrs Davies said.

'No!' the girl said.

Megan turned her head. There was the noise of an aircraft engine. 'Probably one of the RAF out on patrol,' she said.

'No!' Pat whined. 'I heard them every night back home! I know what they sound like!' She dived under the only shelter the house had – the piano.

Megan ran to the kitchen window. Her mother followed. There was a bright flash on the mountainside. Seconds later came the roar of the bomb. The glass rattled in the old frames. 'He's coming up from Swansea!' she called to her mother. 'Dropping his bombs in the fields so he'll get away faster. Don't worry!'

But Megan herself was terrified. This was the dream that she'd had last night. A second flash lit the valley. Closer this time. Then a third.

Megan screamed. 'Mam! Under the piano!'

But Mrs Davies stayed in the kitchen, too terrified to move.

When the bomb hit the house she had no chance.

Megan and Pat survived thanks to the heavy piano. When the young woman woke in hospital they told her the terrible news. Her mother had died.

Megan looked up to the ceiling. 'Oh, God,' she murmured. 'I prayed that I wouldn't have to tell Mam about that dream. Now I never will . . . I never can. Was that your answer to my prayer?'

Did You Know?

1 On Friday 1 September 1939 the service to the 2,000 televisions in Britain was stopped. There was no television again until 1946. Seven years without television . . . today some people can't go seven minutes!

2 Men who joined the armed forces were paid just two shillings (10p) a day at the start of the War. This was increased to three shillings (15p) by the end of the War. Many families were poor and hungry as a result. Some companies and councils paid the men just the same even though they had gone off to fight in the armed forces. (Though one mean council sacked the men so they didn't have to pay them!)

3 Some men didn't have to go off to fight if they didn't want to. Their jobs in Britain were too important. One job considered too important was teaching!

4 Signposts were taken down. The idea was that if enemy soldiers entered the country (or parachuted in) they wouldn't know exactly where they were. Milestones were removed. Shop signs were painted over if they gave a clue as to where they were – 'The Bunchester Bakery' would become 'The ———— Bakery' and so on. As a result a lot of British people got lost! These rules lasted until October 1944.

5 Names of stations were removed from platforms. You didn't know where the train had stopped unless you lived there. A helpful railway poster suggested . . .

6 There was a shortage of beer during the War. And when there was beer to drink there sometimes weren't any glasses to drink it from. In some pubs you could only get a drink if you took your own glass!

7 There was a new dance invented called *The Blackout Stroll*. Take four steps forward, three short steps and a hop . . . then the lights go out. You change partners in the dark and then the lights come on.

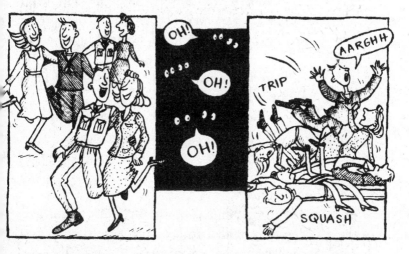

8 If you had more than one dog in the house during an air raid then you were advised to shut them in separate rooms – this was to stop them biting one another in the noise and panic.

9 The Prime Minister, Winston Churchill, wanted to know why people complained about their small meat ration. He was shown a typical meat ration. 'That would be enough for me!' he said. The trouble was he thought he was looking at a day's supply of meat – but it was meant to last a week!

10 Before the War a song was banned because it was too nasty to Germany! It was called, *Even Hitler Had A Mother*. Then, even though Britain was at war, song-writers were nervous about writing anti-German songs.

THE BOTHERSOME BLACKOUT

The British were told that if they showed lights at night then enemy bombers would see the light and drop bombs on them. They were ordered to cover their windows with heavy material if they wanted lights on in a building. Other blackout rules meant:

- street lights were masked to give a pinpoint of light at the base of each lamp post.
- traffic lights were masked to show a small cross of colour
- cars had to drive with a mask over headlights that allowed a tiny slit of light out – their bumpers had to be painted white
- torches had to be pointed down at the pavement and the glass covered with two layers of tissue
- smoking in the street was banned at first – some smokers were even fined for lighting a cigarette during an air-raid warning!
- the tops of pillar-boxes were painted green or yellow. This was so that droplets of deadly mustard gas would stain the paint and show up if there was a gas bomb attack.
- railway carriages were blacked out at first – so you could find yourself sitting on a stranger's knee!

- blacked-out buses were so dim that bus conductors couldn't tell what coins were being handed to them – bus companies found dishonest passengers had slipped them foreign coins when they checked the cash back at the depot.

One railway porter found about the bothersome blackout the hard way: *I fell off the platform last night. Clean over the edge I fell. Mind you, there was a fog at the time.*

Helpful hints for the blackout

1 In the countryside some dark-coloured cows had white lines painted on them in case they wandered on to the road!

2 Men were advised to let their white shirt tails hang out as they walked along the blacked-out roads!

3 Red velvet party cloaks for girls were made with white linings. To walk home in the dark you had to turn them inside out. (There weren't a lot of these cloaks about. More children were killed on roads in the blackout than in peace time even though there were far fewer cars.)

4 Pavements had advice painted in white. The stencil message said 'Walk on left of pavement'. Rather like driving on the left on a road, it helped avoid head-on collisions.

Blackout horrors

Bomber pilots reckoned that even a blacked-out city gave off a glow of light that you couldn't miss from the air. Still, the British people suffered the blackout with some horrible historic results . . .

1 In Peckham, two teenage boys used luminous paint to draw skeletons on dark clothes. In the blackout the paint glowed. Passers-by were terrified!

2 Children in a Cambridge village hid in a churchyard and jumped out on people who had to pass it.

3 Worse things lurked in the London blackout. Just as the dim Victorian streets had hidden Jack the Ripper, so the darkened London streets held the Blackout Ripper. But Jack the Ripper was never caught – Jack the Ripper didn't have a gas mask! George Cummins did . . . and he left it behind at the scene of a nasty attack after he was disturbed. The gas mask had his name in it, and the police traced him easily. He was tried and hanged in 1942.

4 The first planes in an air raid usually dropped fire-bombs. The planes that followed them saw the fires and knew where to drop their high-explosive bombs. So the job of the Air Raid Wardens was to put out these fire-bombs quickly. One string of fire-bombs fell in a London cemetery. The fire watchers rushed to put out the flames. They did this really well. Too well. There was no fire and no light. They stumbled round the graveyard in the pitch darkness, crashed into one another and couldn't find the way out.

5 A girl was going to a dance and had to walk through the blacked-out streets. 'If a strange man talks to you then shine your torch in his eyes, kick him on the shins and run!' her mother told her. The girl set off for the dance. Bins of pig food stood on street corners waiting to be collected. As she rounded a bin a man walked towards her, muffled in a cap and scarf. She shone the torch in his face and kicked his shin. The shocked man fell neck-deep into the pig-bin. The girl ran to the dance. When she reached home her mother whispered to her, 'Your father's a bit upset. Some girl attacked him in the dark - pushed him into that pig-bin on the corner!'

GROTTY GAS MASKS

This poster appeared in 1941:

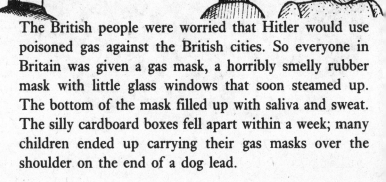

> ## POISON GAS
>
> **1916** THE GERMANS USED POISON GAS
> WE DID NOT EXPECT THIS
> BARBARITY.
>
> **1935** THE ITALIANS USED POISON GAS.
>
> **1941** IT IS YOUR DUTY TO YOURSELF
> YOUR FAMILY AND YOUR
> COUNTRY TO BE PREPARED.
>
> DON'T BE CAUGHT WITHOUT YOUR
> GAS MASK, WHEN THE WARDENS
> SOUND THEIR RATTLES.
>
> DON'T BE A CASUALTY
> —ALWAYS CARRY YOUR GAS MASK—

The British people were worried that Hitler would use poisoned gas against the British cities. So everyone in Britain was given a gas mask, a horribly smelly rubber mask with little glass windows that soon steamed up. The bottom of the mask filled up with saliva and sweat. The silly cardboard boxes fell apart within a week; many children ended up carrying their gas masks over the shoulder on the end of a dog lead.

Gruesome gas facts

1 There were 'gas detectors' placed at street corners. These were supposed to light up if gas was in the air. They were never used. There was never ever a gas bomb attack on Britain . . . yet some people reckon gas masks were one of the great successes of the war! Why? Because Adolf Hitler knew about the gas masks. He knew it would be a waste of time to bomb people with gas when the people were so well prepared – so he didn't bother!

2 Someone invented a gas-proof pram so you could take baby for a walk. It looked a bit like a coffin on wheels with a little chimney to let in gas-free air.

3 The masks made good carriers for children's bottles of school ink or the odd packet of sweets . . . fine, until they had an emergency gas mask practice.

IT'S A GAS MASK MURIEL, NOT A NOSE BAG

MUNCH

4 Gas masks were usually carried in their cardboard boxes. But, if you had some spare money, you could go to a shop and buy a smart carrier made of fancy material. Shops started selling ladies' handbags with special pouches for the gas mask.

5 Men with beards had a real problem with gas masks. One woman managed to fit her husband's head into a gas mask by rolling his beard up with curling pins. But the Cistercian monks, who always wore beards, had no curling pins. They had to shave their beards off.

6 Children were persuaded to wear their masks by making them into 'fun masks'. One of the most common was the red and blue 'Mickey Mouse' mask. Children also discovered that if they wore the mask and blew very hard, the air rushed out of the side and made a very rude noise. The punishment for doing this in school was usually a whack with a cane!

WHO MADE THAT DISGUSTING NOISE?

7 Gas masks had an unusual use. Petrol was in short supply. If you needed some for business you could get it. **But** the special business petrol was stained with red dye – if you cheated and tried to use the red petrol for personal use then you could be caught and fined. Cheats found that if you strained the red petrol through a gas mask filter then it lost the tell-tale colour.

8 People didn't always call them gas masks. Some people called them 'Dickey-birds' (because they made you look as if you had a beak!). They were also known as 'Canaries' and 'Hitlers'. Probably the most common nickname was 'Nosebag'.

9 Some schools held gas mask tests. The children were sent to an air-raid shelter which was then filled with nasty (but not deadly) 'tear gas'. One class survived quite well except for poor little Charlie Bower. He found out the hard way that his mask had a leak – and spent the morning with tears streaming down his face!

10 The War was a time when toys were in short supply. Gas masks made a good toy! You could hold the strap and swing it round your head as a weapon. The metal gas filter could split someone's head open. The pupil with the most dents in their gas mask was seen as a champion.

CATAPULT

DOLL

GOAL POSTS

BAT

True or false: You could buy a gas mask for your dog.

Answer: True. The People's Dispensary for Sick Animals made a gas-proof kennel for dogs, but you could also buy various types of gas masks for them – the best ones were made in Germany!

BLITZED BRIT KIDS

You may think there are boring grown-ups around today. But things haven't changed in the last 50 years. There were some pretty boring people around in the Second World War too. The following advice was given to parents . . . does this sound familiar to you?

Children should:
- be sent to school at the proper times
- be encouraged to 'enjoy' their lessons
- get long hours of sleep
- be given plenty to do
- not be allowed to get over-excited
- understand that 'No' means 'No'

The good news was that the same advice said . . .
Children should:
- be fed at regular hours

The unusual news was that . . .
Children should:
- remember to close gates in the country
- grow to love birds and animals

(So put that cat down at once!)

School secrets

1 The **good** news was that many schools were closed! Many were converted into air raid warden posts. And, of course, 20,000 male teachers went off to fight – even though the law said they didn't have to! (Maybe facing enemy guns was better than facing class 3C on a Friday afternoon!)

2 So, many pupils escaped the terrors of the teachers. In January 1940 only two out of every three children had a school to go to. The **bad** news was that you often spent your holidays working. 'Farm Camps' were set up so that children could 'Lend a hand on the land'.

3 And the **really** bad news, for the young readers of this book, is that a new law was passed in 1944 that meant everyone had to go to secondary school . . . even if you didn't **want** to! And you **still** have to!

4 One school was wrecked by a bomb and 40 children died. The teacher used to take the surviving children round the streets looking for a quiet place to sit and have their lessons on a summer day. They often ended up in the local churchyard, sitting on gravestones. The pupils reckoned that this was so they could be buried quickly if another bomb hit them.

5 A school was wrecked by a land mine one night. Rescuers dug in the rubble and rescued the horrible headmaster and the cruel class teacher. The children were disappointed. But the parents were shocked. What had the headmaster and the teacher been doing alone together in the school at night? 'Fire watching,' the Head said. 'Oh, yes?' said the local people.

World War Two was a frightening time to be a child. You could be evacuated and separated from your parents; you could be sent to live with perfect strangers

– strangers who didn't particularly like you in the first place; you could be separated from your brothers and sisters and your friends. You could also get a bit closer to the fighting, if you really wanted to . . .

The tug-boat tea boy

The British Army landed in France in 1939 and were driven back by the Germans all the way to the coast of northern France near the town of Dunkirk. There weren't enough navy ships to bring the British soldiers home. So a fleet of little private ships and fishing boats set off from England to help.

One of the little boats was a tug-boat from the River Thames. The tea boy was just 14 years old. But he offered to make the trip across the channel and the captain agreed to take him.

When the last soldier had been rescued the little boats sailed home. After 14 days at sea the boy arrived back to a hero's welcome from his proud mother. He took off his socks for the first time in two weeks. They were so stiff with sea salt and dirt that they stood up on their own like a pair of wellington boots.

What did his mother do with those socks?

1 Burn them
2 Keep them as a proud souvenir
3 Wash them

Answer: 2 She kept them and showed them to all of her neighbours. She proudly told them that these were the socks that had been to Dunkirk and back and hadn't been changed once!

But staying in the towns with your family and being blitzed was just as bad as that boy's experience at Dunkirk . . .

Test your teacher

1 Children had to have name tabs sewn into every bit of clothing they had. Was this . . .

a in case the children were lost in the blackout

b in case the clothes were stolen

c in case a child was blown to bits by a bomb and needed to be identified by the clothing

2 How old was the youngest person killed in the war in Britain?

a 11 hours old

b 11 months old

c 11 years old

3 What happened to the 250,000 school meals served each day at the beginning of the War?

a they were abolished

b everyone was encouraged to eat at school and they increased to nearly two million

c they stayed the same

4 Boys had to wear short trousers to save material. When were they allowed to have long trousers?
a when they were over 180 cm tall
b when they were 12 years old
c when they earned enough money to pay for the extra material

5 Because there was a shortage of hand cream something else was suggested to keep your hands smooth and soft. What was it?
a castor sugar rubbed into wet hands
b sandpaper to scrub off the rough bits
c mutton fat rubbed into the hands

6 The WVS appealed for aluminium to help make fighter planes. What did they refuse to accept?
a pots and pans
b the artificial limbs of old soldiers from World War One
c a set of miniature teapots given to Princess Elizabeth by the people of Wales

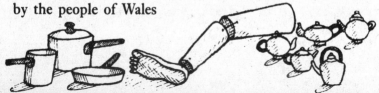

7 Children's groups called Cogs were formed to collect 'salvage' – materials that could be used again for war materials. What was their song?
a 'Whale meat again' to the tune of 'We'll meet again'
b 'It's a long way to Tip a rare pie' to the tune of 'It's a long way to Tipperary'
c 'There'll always be a dustbin' to the tune of 'There'll always be an England'

8 To save fuel the Ministry of Fuel told you how deep to have your bath water. Was it . . .
a 12.7 cm
b 127 cm
c 12.7 inches

9 What was the title of a popular Christmas song in 1939?

a 'Somewhere over the snowman'
b 'Will Santa Claus wear a tin helmet?'
c 'Rudolf the blacked out reindeer'

10 A cartoon character was invented to show the danger of talking to strangers and giving away secrets. Was it . . .
a Mr Chatty
b Tell Tale Tom
c Miss Leaky Mouth

Answers

1 c. 2 a – and the oldest was 100 years old. 3 b. 4 b. 5 a and c. 6 b – pots and pans were collected by the thousand, and the royal miniature teapots were accepted; only the false legs were refused. 7 c. 8 a – or 5 inches if your teacher's old enough to remember them. 9 b. 10 c – slogans included warnings like 'Walls have ears'.

It could have been worse 1

Teachers in Britain had to teach larger classes with fewer materials like paper and pencils. But they were better off than some German teachers. One German child broke his arm. He couldn't give the Hitler salute. The teacher told the boy he needn't bother. But one of the children in the class was a Nazi spy. The teacher was reported to the Nazi Party . . . and executed! (Would you report your teacher? Better not answer that one!)

True or false?

1 The Government urged people to save their milk-bottle tops because there were enough thrown away each year to build a Lancaster bomber.

2 The railways in Britain usually lose money. But in the War they made a lot of money by running fewer trains and cramming more people into them.

IS THERE ROOM FOR A LITTLE ONE?

3 An RAF pilot wanted seven gallons of petrol to go home in his car on leave. He was refused . . . so he flew home in his Spitfire instead.

4 The readers of the comic *Hotspur* raised £700,000 to buy a warship, *HMS Hotspur*, for the navy.

5 One of the hobby clubs you could join after school taught how to keep pigs.

6 Farmers kept manure in small heaps around the edge of the fields. The manure was good for putting out fires.

7 Soldiers writing home had very little space on their cards so they used short forms like SWALK. This meant, 'Soldiers Will Always Love the King'.

8 Munitions factories (which made shells, bullets and explosives) were disguised as duck ponds so that enemy bombers couldn't pick them out.

ZEY MUST THINK WE ARE QUACKERS

9 Rationing finished when the War ended in 1945.

10 People who died in air raids were the responsibility of the Government's Ministry of Health.

Answers

1 False – the government claimed that wasted milk-bottle tops would build fifty Lancaster bombers!

2 True – the railway posters tried to put rail travellers off by asking, 'Is your Journey Really Necessary?' Then, if people still went ahead, they were told not to mind if the train was late or crowded (or both!). 'Food, shells and fuel must come first.' The suffering public agreed!

3 True – and he used 280 gallons instead.

4 False – it was a football club that raised the money. Which club? Tottenham Hotspur, of course.

5 True – other hobby clubs taught you how to mend clothes or repair shoes.

6 True – you could keep it round the edge of the school playing fields in case your school caught fire . . . then again you might have preferred to let the school burn! Manure was also used by horrible wartime children – they threw it at German Prisoners of War!

7 False – Soldiers **did** write home with SWALK on the envelope . . . but the letters stood for 'Sealed With A Loving Kiss'.

8 True – the 'pond' was painted on. And ducks were painted swimming on it.

9 False – many things stayed on ration until 1954.

10 True – The Ministry of Health also looked after home repairs.

Blitzed books

Like everything else, paper was in short supply during World War Two. Millions of old books were turned into pulp to make new books. But the only new books to be published were ones that were sure to sell. For children, that meant books by writers like Enid Blyton.

Here's a story in old Enid's style. The only difference is that the facts in it are true . . .

The Curious Case of the Kit Kat

'I say, Janet, I'm jolly hungry,' Bobby groaned. Bobby, short for Roberta, rubbed her tummy.

'I know,' Janet sighed. 'Cook dished up that awful dried egg again this morning. It's getting jolly boring!'

The girls took out their books and went to their desks. 'Gosh, Janet! What's this tin box doing on my desk?' Bobby asked.

'I don't know, Bobby. But I've got one too!' Janet cried.

'Perhaps it's a bomb from those beastly Germans!' Bobby said. Bobby always liked to make an adventure out of everything. 'Shall we open it and see?'

'No!' Janet squealed. 'Look at that label on the lid!'

Bobby read it carefully. 'Do not open except in an emergency!' Bobby was a good reader. 'How odd! I wish I could look inside!'

'Miss Grant would be furious,' Janet warned her chum. 'You don't want another two hours of prep, do you? You'd miss the house hockey match!'

Bobby sighed. 'It would almost be worth it to solve the mystery.'

Just then Miss Grant marched in. Her back was straight as a poker and her thin face as sharp as a pin. The girls stood up. Miss Grant glared at them. 'Good morning, form 3A.'

'Good morning, Miss Grant,' the girls replied.

'Sit!'

The girls sat. Miss Grant pulled herself up to her full height. 'Now, girls, you're probably wondering what's inside the tin boxes on your desks.'

'Yes, Miss Grant.'

'Well, I can tell you, they are emergency rations. Your parents were asked to send them. If there's an enemy attack and our kitchens are destroyed, then the food in this box will keep you going for a day or two until help arrives,' the tall teacher explained. She looked fiercely down her thin nose at Bobby. 'You must not open these boxes. Ever! Do you understand?'

'Yes, Miss Grant,' Bobby said. Then she whispered to her pal, Janet, 'Why is she looking at me?'

'Because everyone knows what a jolly greedy little carrot you are!' Janet whispered back.

The next morning Bobby received a letter from her mother. She read it to Janet. 'Oh! I say, Janet! Mummy says she's put a bar of Kit Kat chocolate in that box. I have to have it! I'll die if I don't have a bite!'

'And you'll die if Miss Grant catches you looking in the box. Don't you jolly well dare open that box!' her friend warned her.

Suddenly there was the sound of a bell clanging in the corridor outside the classroom. 'Air-raid practice!' Miss Grant said sharply. 'Let's see if we can beat last week's time of two minutes and thirty-five seconds to the shelter, shall we? And don't forget your gas masks!'

The girls stood. One row at a time they walked smartly from the room. Miss Grant looked at her watch. As they reached the end of the corridor Bobby stopped suddenly. 'Oh, lor!' she gasped. 'I've gone and forgotten my secret box! Old Grunt will kill me! She'll make me miss the hockey match for sure.'

Janet grabbed her arm. 'Don't worry. I'll go back and get it. You take mine.'

'You'll cop it off Grunt!' Bobby cried.

'Don't worry, Bobs. That's what friends are for!' Janet said bravely and turned back.

As she hurried back to the classroom she saw Miss Grant standing there. In the teacher's thin hands was Bobby's box. 'Forgotten something?' Miss Grant snapped.

'Er, yes, Miss Grant. I forgot my emergency rations,' Janet said.

'I have it here,' the teacher said. 'Take it . . . but don't dare open it! And you can have two hours extra prep tonight.'

'I'll miss the house hockey match,' Janet pleaded.

'I know,' Miss Grant said with a wintry smile. 'And let that be a lesson to you.'

Janet nodded and turned away. Miss Grant didn't notice that the girl was smiling. Janet knew that Bobby was the best hockey player in the house. Fast as a boy and nearly as tough. So long as Bobby played the house was sure to win.

* * *

That night in the dormitory Bobby waited till after lights-out. She crept across the room to Janet's bed with the tin box clutched in her hand. 'Janet,' she whispered.

'Is that you, Bobby?' the girl asked.

'Yes. Look, Janet, how about a midnight feast to celebrate the win at hockey?'

'Oh, yes, the skipper said your five goals were

absolutely super. Well done, Bobs. But where will we get the food from?'

Bobby grinned. 'We'll eat the emergency rations!'

'Oh, no, Bobby! You'd get into terrible trouble!'

'We won't, silly! If we aren't supposed to open them then no one will ever know!'

Bobby fumbled with her torch and clicked it on. The other girls in the dorm gathered round and watched as Bobby opened the box. There was a gasp from every girl. 'Ooooh!' Janet squeaked. 'The Kit Kat! It's missing! It's been stolen!'

'Hmmm,' Bobby nodded and looked around. 'And I think I know the culprit!'

But do you? Who stole the Kit Kat? Was it . . .

1 Bobby herself
2 Janet, who had rescued the box from the classroom
3 one of the girls in the dormitory
4 the teacher

Answer: 4 – In the true story the girl opened the box. She then told the teacher the precious chocolate bar was missing. The teacher turned bright red. Everyone then knew who'd stolen it.
Would your teacher do a thing like that?

EVILS OF EVACUATION

The British expected their cities to be bombed. So, long before the war, plans were made to move the children out to foster homes in the countryside. As soon as war was declared they went by train and bus into the unknown. Very often they went together with their teachers who carried on with the same classes in a quiet country school. The two most common methods of finding a new home were . . .

The Slave Market – the children stood in a group. The people who were offering homes then picked the ones they wanted. Tidy, polite little girls went first - scruffy, smelly little boys were wanted by no one.

Hunt the house – children were led around the town or village. The house-owners were asked, 'Would you like to take this one?'

Finding someone you'd be happy with was usually a matter of luck. Some evacuees were so happy they didn't want to go home after the War . . . some still say their evacuation days were the happiest days of their lives. Some hosts made friendships with their guests that have lasted a lifetime.

But there were also some problems. Children born and raised in the city slums of the 1930s found the countryside as strange as you'd find living on Mars! These were the . . .

Problem kids

Some of the problems the new homes had with evacuees included . . .

● Home sickness – 'My name is Bobby,' the three-year old boy wept. 'I'm a big boy, and I don't cry – well, not very often!'

● Bed-wetting – some estimates say that one evacuee in three suffered from bed-wetting.

● Nits – some of the children from the poorer parts of the cities evacuated their head-lice with them.

• Dirt – some children were not used to regular baths. One pair of evacuees screamed the house down when they were stripped in the bathroom . . . they thought they were going to be drowned!

• Clothing – poor city children were often 'Plastered up' for the winter. That is, they had brown paper or newspaper wrapped around their bodies to keep them warm. The paper was then held in place for the winter by a vest that was sewn up tight. When warmer weather came, next spring, the stinking vest would be cut off and the paper removed . . . along with the body lice that had usually found a nice snug home in there!

• Swearing – some of the rougher evacuees shocked the foster parents in small towns who weren't used to hearing children swear. One evacuee dropped a fork and swore. 'You shouldn't use words like that,' she was told.

'I'll tell my dad about you,' she replied. 'An' he'll come an' knock your *!*!*!*! block off!'

In September 1939, as soon as war was declared, one and a half million women and children were evacuated to the country for safety. But, when the enemy bombers didn't arrive as expected, a lot went back home. By January 1940 nearly a million had returned to the towns and cities.

Some of the smaller towns were so empty for a while that they became like ghost towns. In Margate, grass grew in the streets.

Six true tales of evacuees

1 Some evacuees brought bad habits from the town to the country. Some went shopping then came back with the goods . . . and the money! To the horror of the host they'd shoplifted them! Another family of evacuees pretended to dig in the garden to grow vegetables. In fact they were digging a tunnel into next-door's garden. They pinched the potatoes they found underground there. The neighbours saw the leaves of the plants still growing and didn't discover the theft until they came to pull them up in the autumn!

2 One evacuee was criticised for spilling her tea:

3 A mother went into the country to visit her little three-year-old daughter and baby son. The little girl she met was her daughter – but the baby boy was not her son! The two children had arrived two months earlier. 'It says on this paper that you have your brother with you,' one of the welcoming women had said. 'Where is he?' The little girl looked around then pointed to a toddler who was not her brother. It seemed that she didn't like her baby brother so she had picked one that she preferred!

4 A boy was sent to a huge manor house owned by a grand lady. He thought he'd escaped the bombing and the shooting. He was terrified to hear shots one day coming from inside the house! He rushed into the living-room to find the lady with a smoking shotgun pointed through an open window.

'Got him!' she said.

'A German?'

'No! A grey squirrel! I hate the things. Every time I see one in my garden I shoot the blighter!'

5 There are many stories of city evacuees being amazed at the sight of farm animals. They'd never left the city and never seen a cow or a sheep or a chicken before – except cooked and carved at the dinner table. In October 1939 the BBC News broadcast this description of a cow. It was written by a young evacuee. Could you picture a cow from this description?

The cow is a mammal. It has six sides: right, left, upper and below. At the back it has a tail on which hangs a brush. With this it sends flies away so they do not fall into the milk. The head is for the purpose of growing horns and so that the mouth can be somewhere. The horns are to butt with and the mouth is to moo with. Under the cow hangs the milk. It is arranged for milking. When people milk the milk comes and there is never an end to the supply. How the cow does it I have not realised but it makes more and more. The cow has a fine sense of smell; one can smell it far away. This is the reason for fresh air in the country. The man cow is called an ox. It is not a mammal. The cow does not eat much, but what it eats it eats twice so that it gets enough. When it is hungry it moos and when it says nothing it is because it is all full up with grass.

6 A girl evacuee loved gingerbread. Her strict hostess cooked some one day and left it to cool. While the woman was asleep the girl crept into the kitchen and nipped a bit from the side of one of the tempting pieces. This made the cake look odd, so the girl had a bright idea. If she nipped a piece from every single cake, then the hostess would not notice one odd one. It didn't work! The hostess lined up her evacuees and asked who had done it. The girl's guilty looks gave her away. Her punishment was to be locked in a cold, damp attic. Quite by chance her mother arrived on a visit later that day. She was so shocked by the treatment of her daughter that she took her straight home.

World War Three! – Hosts v Evacuees
Which was worse . . . being an evacuee, or being a host in the country who had the job of living with the evacuees? There are two sides to every argument. This is what the hosts said . . .
1 Host: You couldn't buy a small-tooth comb anywhere in Northallerton. They'd all been bought because a lot of the evacuees came with fleas in their hair.
2 Host's daughter: I came home from work one day and found two youths, nearly as tall as my father. They'd told mother we had to take them because we had a spare bedroom.
3 Host's daughter: There were five of us in a three-bedroom house. When we took an evacuee it meant my brother had to share my bedroom. I resented this, as I took an instant dislike to the lad who came to stay with us.

4 Host's daughter: Our evacuees arrived in shabby clothes so mother gave them new ones. They were allowed home on a visit and came back with more old clothes. Their parents had sold the new ones we'd given them!

5 Host's daughter: Our new evacuee was a terror. One day he was playing with matches and he set fire to a chair. We had to decorate after he left. The door was covered with dart holes and the walls with writing.

6 Hostess: My father used to say he never saw anything like our evacuees – they never shed a tear when their parents left for home.

7 Hostess: We had three brothers aged four to eight. They had no idea of food other than chips. They didn't know how to eat a boiled egg.

BUT some said . . .

8 Host's daughter: My parents took a boy of 6. He was really a wonderful child in every way. He was brought up by my parents as one of the family. His mother came and stayed long weekends and holidays with us.

On the other hand, this is what the evacuees said . . .

1 Girl evacuee aged seven: The farm was three miles from the village and had only cold water which had to be pumped up into the kitchen.

2 Girl evacuee aged seven: The toilet was at the end of a long garden and was just a pit in the ground filled with ashes. It had two holes. The farmer's daughter and I always went together, particularly in the dark.

3 Girl evacuee: I remember my eleventh birthday. Mrs Spencer took me seven miles to see *Tarzan of the Apes*. But there was only a bus there. We had to walk back.

4 Girl evacuee aged nine: We fed the chickens each day. I thought they were pets and was heartbroken when I saw the first one killed and plucked. I once witnessed the slaughter of a pig. It was so distressing that I started having nightmares. I was firmly told that this was their way of life. I was a very silly, spoilt child who knew nothing.

5 Girl evacuee aged seven: One thing that upset me was that the only farm worker was not allowed to sit at the table with the family. He had to have his meal at a separate table.

6 Boy evacuee aged twelve: There were lots of apple and pear orchards. We thought you could just help yourself. The village kids told us we shouldn't do it. The police came to see our hosts and they put a stop to it.

7 Girl evacuee aged nine: Anything wrong in the house was always my fault because the farmer's daughters ganged together. They broke my only doll and tore my books. When mum collected me she was in tears. She could see every bone in my body.

BUT some had happy memories . . .

8 Girl evacuee aged eight: We helped on the farm at weekends. I used to like watching the milking done. It was done by hand. We used to love the lambing season when we could go and see the lambs after they were born. It was all new to us. In the town we only had factories and shipyards.

Marjorie's story

On 2 May 1945 evacuation was ended everywhere. Hull and London were the last places to have children returned because they were the most dangerous. Saddest of all were the children who were evacuated and never got to go back home. Some had no homes to go back to – they'd been blitzed. But some found that their parents had moved – and abandoned their children. About 38,000 children were unclaimed after the War.

ROTTEN RATIONING

Rationing was brought in by the Government to save food and materials and make sure everyone got fair shares. Everyone was given **coupons**. You had to have so many coupons for each rationed thing you bought. It usually worked well. But some people cheated.

1 One shop-keeper was a blind old woman. Children made their own coupons out of blotting paper. To the blind woman it felt like a coupon so she handed over the sweets!

2 If you'd run out of coupons but had plenty of money then you could buy something illegally – and hope to get away with it. The practice of selling things this way was known as 'the black market'.

3 One man called himself The Sugar Baron. His job was to send the precious sugar supplies to shops. The Government knew how much he was sent and checked that he had given it all to the shops to ration to the people. But he started giving shops short measures and holding some back. Or he 'accidentally' dropped a bag. This way he built up a private supply which he could sell for a lot of money or swap for something he needed. Even 50 years later he wasn't sorry for cheating his fellow-Britons. 'Everybody did it if they got the chance,' he said. 'Life was hard. You had to grab what you could when you could.'

4 Clothes were rationed in 1941, but by 1942 the rules for making clothes became crazy:

● men's suits could only have three pockets

- men's suits could only have three buttons on the front and none on the cuff
- fancy belts were banned
- trouser legs couldn't be wider than 19 inches (48 cm) at the bottom
- elastic waistbands were banned
- turn-ups on the bottom of trousers were banned. (You got round this one by finding a tailor who would make your trousers too long – he'd then be allowed to turn them up to make them fit. Crazy!)
- high heels on shoes were to be no more than two inches (5 cm)

5 Of course it was hard to be fair. You needed two coupons for a pair of knickers. But if a woman was fatter than average, or preferred knickers with longer legs (bloomers), then she needed more precious elastic – she'd have to fork out **three** coupons.

6 Of course a death in the family was a very sad thing but you could always take the dead person's old clothes and use the material to make new ones for you and your family. Or, if you didn't like wearing their clothes, you might find the dear deceased person's clothing coupons and spend them quickly before the Government inspectors found out they were dead. (The law said you couldn't use your coupons after you were dead . . . which seems fair enough.)

7 Petrol rationing allowed you to drive about 20 to 50 miles (32 to 80km) a week. But sharing cars saved money. If you put up a sign in your car window offering people lifts then you could get extra petrol.

ROOM FOR ANOTHER LITTLE ONE?

One way round the petrol ration was to fill a bag with household gas and adapt your car to run on it. The **good** news was that town gas was not rationed. The **bad** news was . . .

THE GAS BAG WAS 3 METRES LONG 2 METRES WIDE AND OVER 1 METRE HIGH NEARLY AS BIG AS THE CAR

SO....

IT HAD TO BE CARRIED ON THE ROOF

BUT....

AS THE BAG EMPTIED IT DROOPED OVER THE WINDOWS

SO....

IT HAD TO BE HELD IN A CRATE

BUT....

THE CRATE WAS SO HEAVY IT MADE THE CAR HARD TO DRIVE

AND....

IT COST £30 TO BUY AND FIT THE GAS BAG AT A TIME WHEN A NEW CAR COST ONLY £100

YET....

ALL THAT GAS GAVE YOU AS MANY MILES AS JUST 1 GALLON OF PETROL (4·5 LITRES)

THEN....

IT TOOK 10 MINUTES TO REFILL THE GAS BAG EVERY 20 MILES (32 km) OR SO

AND....

GAS BECAME IN SHORT SUPPLY IN OCTOBER 1942

SO....

WAS IT WORTH IT?

8 After petrol for private motoring was stopped in 1942 you could claim that you needed petrol for a very

important journey. If you got the petrol then you had to make the journey by the shortest possible route. A business-man who went 1200 metres out of his way to pop home for lunch was fined . . . and he was lucky! A writer of theatre musicals (Ivor Novello) used his car to go home every night after the show . . . he was given four weeks in jail!

9 Coal was rationed. Families who ran out of coal often turned on the gas oven, opened the oven door and sat round it. They even put their feet in the oven to try to get warm!

10 Cigarettes were in such short supply that shops often worked out their own rationing. They would sell just one packet to each customer. One ruthless father got his two children out of bed at 5:00 a.m. each morning and sent each to queue at a different tobacconist shop for his Winston cigarettes. That way he got double supply. But that wasn't good enough. As soon as they brought home the cigarettes he sent them out again and they swapped queues so they could each have a second packet. He got four packets a day this way! He wouldn't get away with it today – children aren't allowed to buy cigarettes!

It could have been worse 2

. . . you could have been living in Germany! Germany brought in rationing before the war even started. Two particularly harsh laws said:

- citizens were only allowed to take a bath on a Saturday or a Sunday
- citizens could only buy toilet paper from a 'Toilet Paper Distribution Centre' – this was to stop the precious stuff being stolen

Match the clothes to the coupons

Clothes coupons were needed according to the amount of material and the amount of work that went into making the clothes. You only had 66 coupons to last you a year – less as the War went on. If you were a government officer in charge of sharing out coupons, how many would you give for each of these items?

1 a night-dress   4 underpants

2 a man's overcoat   5 a handkerchief

3 a dress   6 pyjamas

The coupons you'd need to get the above are:
16, 11, 8, 6, 4 or a half . . . but which needs which?

The tale of the undressed dancer

There's a story in the Bible about a dancer called Salome. Salome wore seven thin pieces of cloth. She then did a rather rude dance in which she took off the veils one by one! King Herod was so pleased he gave her a present . . . the head of John the Baptist. On a plate! (There's no accounting for taste.)

This dance was so famous that lots of women have copied *The Dance of the Seven Veils* throughout the centuries. A dancer even performed it during the blitz to entertain soldiers. It was a bit naughty, but the police couldn't stop her.

Rationing did! As she took the veils off she threw them into the audience . . . but never got them back.

And she didn't have the coupons to go out and buy new 'veils', so she had to give up the act!

73

(Yes, we know she **could** have bought blackout material without using her precious coupons . . . but *The Dance of the Seven Blackout Curtains* just isn't the same.)

Rotten war for women

The good news . . .
With working men fighting in the army, more women had to go out to work. They wore their trousers with pride! It showed they were part of the war effort. They had more freedom than ever before.

The bad news . . .
- women wore tighter clothes to save material.
- sleeveless sweaters were worn.
- pleats were banned . . . they wasted material and machine time.

74

• if a woman wanted a white wedding dress she had to make it herself ... sometimes out of silk left over from making parachutes! No parachutes? Then use a satin table-cloth or a net curtain.

• After the War many women gave up the freedom they'd won in the War. They gave up the trousers and went back to fashion clothes.

• Rationing went on until 1952. The new fashions, like Dior's 'New Look', demanded lots of material. Women who couldn't afford the money or the coupons for the 'New Look' resented the women who could. In 1947 women wearing the 'New Look' had their clothes ripped off in the street by other women!

75

ROTTEN RATIONED RECIPES

Any food supply that came to Britain in ships was in danger of being cut off. Enemy submarines in the Atlantic sank as many food ships as they could. They hoped to starve Britain into surrendering. The British Government had two main answers to this.

1 Make sure that no one eats more than a fair share of the food we have – give everyone a Ration Book with coupons to allow you to have so much each week and no more.

2 Persuade everyone to eat the type of food there was plenty of in Britain. Food like potatoes.

The Minister of Food was Lord Woolton. He told the British people:

THIS IS A FOOD WAR. IF WE GROW MORE POTATOES THEN WE NEED NOT IMPORT MUCH WHEAT. THE VEGETABLE GARDEN IS ALSO OUR NATIONAL MEDICINE CHEST. THE BATTLE ON THE KITCHEN FRONT CANNOT BE WON WITHOUT HELP FROM THE KITCHEN GARDEN.

How do you persuade someone to eat more potatoes?

- Well, you could try writing a jolly jingle like
  this one . . .

THE SONG OF POTATO PETE
POTATOES NEW POTATOES OLD
POTATOES (IN A SALAD) COLD
POTATOES BAKED OR MASHED OR FRIED
POTATOES WHOLE, POTATOES PIED
ENJOY THEM ALL, INCLUDING CHIPS
REMEMBERING SPUDS DON'T COME IN SHIPS!

(If the potatoes were as bad as the poetry then you
wouldn't want to eat them!)

- you could try persuading people that potatoes are
  the best food in the world . . .

*Potatoes help to protect you from illness. Potatoes give you
warmth and energy. Potatoes are cheap and home-produced.
So why stop at serving them just once a day? Have them
twice, or even three times, for breakfast, dinner and supper.*

(If you followed all this advice you'd probably end up
looking like a potato! Come to think of it some people
do . . . well, most of us have a couple of eyes and a
jacket.)

- and you could come up with scrumptious recipes
  that will use up those endless spuds . . .

'FADGE' IS HOT NOURISHING AND FILLING FOR BREAKFAST

BOIL SOME WELL SCRUBBED POTATOES, THEN PEEL AND MASH THEM WHILE HOT. WHEN THE MIXTURE IS COOL ENOUGH TO HANDLE ADD SALT, AND WORK IN ENOUGH FLOUR TO MAKE A PLIABLE DOUGH. KNEAD LIGHTLY ON A WELL-FLOURED BOARD FOR ABOUT 5 MINUTES THEN ROLL INTO A LARGE CIRCLE ABOUT 1/4 INCH (1/2 cm) THICK. CUT INTO WEDGE SHAPED PIECES AND COOK ON A HOT GRIDDLE, AN ELECTRIC HOT-PLATE OR ON THE UPPER SHELF OF A QUICK OVEN UNTIL BROWN ON BOTH SIDES. TURNING ONCE.

(Why not make this Fadge recipe . . . then try it on someone you don't like?)

● the Government even tried to persuade you to eat the bits you usually threw away!

THOSE WHO HAVE THE WILL TO WIN
COOK POTATOES IN THEIR SKIN
KNOWING THAT THE SIGHT OF PEELINGS
DEEPLY HURT LORD WOOTTON'S FEELINGS

SPLUTTER
SPLUTTER

(So, if you saw a man crying over a bin of pig swill it may well have been Lord Woolton!)

War time recipes you may like to try

TWO-MINUTE SOUP

INGREDIENTS

4 TABLESPOONS DRIED MILK (60 ml)

1 BEEF OR VEGETABLE STOCK CUBE

2 TABLESPOONS PARSLEY (30 ml)

A PINCH OF SALT

METHOD

1 MIX THE DRIED MILK WITH 2 TABLESPOONS OF WATER AND BEAT HARD WITH A WOODEN SPOON (OR WHISK) UNTIL IT IS SMOOTH. ADD THE REST OF THE WATER AND MIX WELL

2 PUT IN A PAN AND HEAT. BRING TO BOIL AND STIR IN THE STOCK CUBE, THE PARSLEY AND THE SALT.

3 BOIL GENTLY AND STIR FOR FIVE MINUTES SERVE WITH BREAD

COD PANCAKES

INGREDIENTS

225g COD (COOKED AND FLAKED)

15g PARSLEY (CHOPPED)

30g MIXED HERBS

175g MASHED CARROTS

PINCH OF SALT AND PEPPER

FOR THE BATTER.

25g PLAIN FLOUR

15g DRIED EGG (1 LEVEL TEASPOON)

5g BAKING POWDER (2 TEASPOONS)

HALF PINT OF WATER (800 ml)   CONT....

METHOD.

1. MIX TOGETHER ALL THE DRY INGREDIENTS FOR THE BATTER. ADD SUFFICIENT WATER TO MAKE STIFF DOUGH.
2. BEAT WELL AND ADD THE REST OF THE WATER
3. MIX COD, CARROTS, PARSLEY AND HERBS WITH THE BATTER
4. HEAT A FRYING PAN AND ADD A LITTLE FAT.
5. PLACE THE PANCAKE MIXTURE IN THE PAN
6. COOK EACH SIDE UNTIL BROWN. SERVE WITH POTATOES

Ten foul food facts

1 Suggested new recipes included squirrel-tail soup and crow pie.

2 A competition for good food in the *Farmer & Stock Breeder* magazine was won with recipes for fried bullock brains and lamb's-tail broth.

3 It was an offence to give bread to birds – but birds survived. One farmer used hops from the local brewery instead of manure and spread it over his crops. The birds pinched the brewed hops – and got very drunk.

4 Rabbits made a good dinner – yes, even fluffy little pet rabbits – and the skins left over made nice warm gloves.

5 Dead horses were sold as dog food – but the flesh was dyed green to stop people selling it for beef steaks. (Luckily dogs are colour-blind!) Bones were collected in bins on the corners of streets. Meat bones were a source of nitroglycerine for high explosives, glue for aircraft, food for cattle and fertiliser for crops. Many a dog had a feast there . . . hopefully it didn't explode.

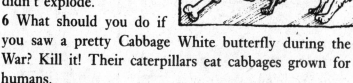

6 What should you do if you saw a pretty Cabbage White butterfly during the War? Kill it! Their caterpillars eat cabbages grown for humans.

7 Shortage of meat meant that sausages often had curious things in them. One woman complained that her sausages had so much bread in them they turned to toast when they were cooked. *We didn't know whether to put mustard on them or marmalade!*

8 War children had never seen a banana. They didn't know how to eat one. There are many stories of children trying to eat them skins and all. Others peeled them correctly – then threw the inside away and ate the skin!

81

9 A suggestion was made for a wartime type of 'banana' – boil up turnips, then let them go cold. Mash them with sugar and you had something that tasted like banana. (You can try it – if you fancy a day off school with terminal sickness.)

10 It could have been worse. In some countries food was rationed depending on what job you had. Important people got better food. 'Nobodies' got next to nothing!

You could always go to a restaurant and eat without coupons. But it was an expensive way to eat – and the helpings were not very big . . .

The Tale of the Chocolate Dog

Sammy was a sailor. Like many sailors he was very superstitious. He never walked under a ladder and never broke a mirror.

As he left his London home one morning he met a mongrel mutt called Mick. 'Hello, Mick!' the sailor said. He reached down and patted the rough, grey coat. Mick wagged his tail.

Sammy reached into his pocket and found a small piece of chocolate. He threw it in the air. Mick caught it and trotted back to the O'Malley family home chewing it happily.

'Hello, Mick,' Mrs O'Malley smiled. 'Been at the bone-bin again, have you?'

Mick just wagged his tail happily.

Sammy the sailor forgot about his gift to Mick. He set sail with a convoy into the Atlantic. The weather was calm and the crew were nervous. Enemy submarines, the dreaded U-boats, would have a clear target for their torpedoes.

After three days at sea the alarm siren sounded. Sammy grabbed a rifle and rushed to his battle station at the front of the ship. The submarine periscope was just vanishing below the water. A ripple of white foam was rushing towards the ship. A torpedo!

The captain was desperately trying to turn the ship away from the deadly missile. But it was turning too slowly and too late. The torpedo rushed towards Sammy. He knew it was the end. The sailor raised the rifle to his shoulder and tried to aim at the torpedo. If he could hit the warhead before it struck the ship then he'd be saved.

But the ship rose and fell in the water. Sammy closed his eyes. He fired.

There was a shattering explosion. A plume of white water. Spray stung Sammy's face. Then there was a curious silence. Sammy opened his eyes. The water was bubbling about fifty metres from the ship.

The crew walked towards Sammy and looked at him with wonder. 'That was the best shot I've ever seen!' the ship's cook said.

Sammy shook his head then found his voice. 'Not a good shot – just luck!'

The cook shrugged. 'Then I wish I had a piece of your rabbit's foot or your four-leaf clover, Sammy.'

Suddenly Sammy had a clear picture in his mind. 'Mick! The dog! They do say, stroke a lucky dog and the luck will rub off.'

'Then give it a pat from me,' the cook said.

'I gave it a piece of chocolate,' Sammy said.

'I've lots of chocolate in the galley. Give it the

biggest slab I can find! It's just saved all our lives!'

And so, just two weeks later, Mick the mongrel had a fortune in rare chocolate in his slobbering chops. He wagged his tail so hard you'd have thought it would fall off.

'Hello, Mick!' Mrs O'Malley said. 'What have we got here? Drop! Good boy, Mick. Drop!' She picked up the dark brown bar and wiped it on her apron. 'Well, well, well! Mr O'Malley always said you were a lucky dog! Here, I'll give you a nice old bone!'

Mick trotted off with his reward and his mistress set to work with a carving knife.

Christmas that year was a good one for John and Lucy, Tony and Arthur, the little O'Malleys. They opened their presents and almost cried with pleasure as they saw their treats.

'Oh, Ma! That was beautiful!' Lucy said as her mother tucked her into the bed under the steel table. 'How did you get all that chocolate, Ma?'

'Ask no questions and you'll be told no lies,' her mother said.

'I think it was carried here by Santa's reindeer. The clever thing carried it in his mouth,' Lucy whispered.

'And why do you think that?'

The little girl said softly, 'Because my slab of chocolate was covered in teeth marks!'

THE BLACK MARKET

People often had money to spare – there wasn't enough food, clothing, cars, entertainment or furniture to spend it on. And of course rationing meant you could only have so much food, petrol or clothes anyway.

So, if you had something that was in short supply – and you knew someone with money who wanted it – you could sell it to them without coupons.

This was against the law, you understand. But if you could get away with it you could make a lot of illegal money. This wasn't an open market – so it was known as the black market. For some people the black market was the chance to make a little extra cash. For others it was a way of life . . .

Death in the Haystack – the true story of Jack Lapham.

Jack Lapham supped his pint of beer carefully. It was going to have to last him all evening. He didn't mind. It was the company in The Grey Horse that he liked.

Bill Anderson the barman leaned over the counter and murmured, 'I could top that pint up for you, Jack.'

Jack drew in his breath sharply. 'Thanks, Bill, but no thanks. We're all in this war together. If we don't share and share alike then we may as well let the Germans take over tomorrow. Besides, I'm on duty later tonight. It doesn't do to let the villagers see their Special Constable rolling round drunk, does it?'

Bill laughed. 'The amount of crime we have here in Farlington, I don't think it matters!'

The Special Constable shook his grey-haired head seriously. 'You never know, Bill. You never know.'

A chill draught swept into the bar as the door opened and a stranger hurried into the bar. The young man had dark hair that was parted in the centre and greased flat to his thin skull. He was carrying a brown paper carrier-bag under his arm.

'Good evening, sir. What can I get you?' Bill Anderson asked.

'Nuffin,' the young stranger croaked in a hoarse voice. He jabbed a grubby finger at the parcel. 'It's more a case of what I can get for you!'

'Ah, a case of whisky would come in handy.'

'Nah!' the young man scowled. He looked suspiciously at Jack Lapham and nodded for Bill to join him at the quiet corner of the bar.

Even though he spoke in that soft, croaking voice Jack Lapham could hear most of what the stranger said. 'Nice bit of beef . . . fresh as a daisy . . . ten shillings!'

'No coupons,' the barman shrugged.

'Nah! Don't need none. Nice bit of beef. Cook it. Serve beef sandwiches to the customers, eh? Just nine shillings to you, guv!'

'Probably dog meat,' Bill sniffed.

'Hah! I'll give yer dog meat! Killed just down the road. Fresh as a daisy!' The young man's red-rimmed eyes narrowed. 'I can sell this for twice the price in London, mate!'

'Then good luck to you,' the barman sniffed and turned to polish a glass.

'Yer'll be sorry,' the stranger snapped and scuttled out of the bar.

Bill Anderson met the eyes of his old friend. 'You hear that, Jack?'

'I heard, Bill.'

'Surprised you didn't arrest him.'

'I'm not in me uniform yet . . . besides, I'm more interested in finding out who's supplying this meat.'

Bill rubbed his stubbled chin – new razors were hard to find these days. 'My money would be on those Wades – a shifty family if ever I saw one.'

'I'll start there,' Jack Lapham promised. He drained the last of his beer, put his cap on and set off to change into his uniform.

The blackout had begun by the time he wheeled his bicycle down the track to Farlington Marsh Farm. The slit in his front lamp gave next to no light and the thin moon was little help. The Special Constable cursed as he stumbled along the rutted track, ankle deep in mud and with overhanging brambles snatching at his hat.

The farm gate was slippery with moss as he pushed it open. There was no light at the farmhouse windows – Jack would have been upset if he'd seen any. Some of these farmers were careless about blackout. They knew the Air Raid Precaution wardens would never venture this far out.

Jack propped his bike against the farmhouse wall. He took his bike lamp and shone it into the farmhouse window. There were no shutters or curtains there. It was deserted. And as he inspected the barns he realised there was little hay or straw in there.

In the field behind the barn was a haystack with a waterproof cover. Nothing here to suggest a slaughterhouse.

He stumbled against an empty oil drum and cursed the darkness. He stopped to rub his knee. Then he realized the darkness was in fact his biggest friend. Because although he could see nothing his ears were sharpened.

There were owls in the distant woods. Odd scuttlings of rats in the barn. But there was another noise from behind the barn. Someone was sawing. Jack strained his ears and crept to the back of the barn. The soft sawing wasn't like the cutting of wood. It was the sawing of bones that he'd heard in the butcher shop.

The sawing stopped for a few moments. There was the sound of men talking, then a chopping. Jack walked along the side of the haystack and looked carefully round the corner. The wafer-thin moon lit the flat field. It was empty!

Now the sound of sawing came from behind the Special Constable. He hurried along the edge of the haystack, turned the corner and found himself looking into the deserted farmyard. For a moment Jack thought he was hearing ghosts and was ready to run for his cycle. Then he heard a loud, clear laugh from his left. From the haystack. And he realized that the sounds were coming from *inside* the stack.

Using his torch he walked carefully along the side of the stack. Bales of hay had been stacked against the side of a wooden building to disguise it. But he found the door and opened it quietly.

The light from the oil lamps was brilliant as he stepped inside from the deep purple of the night. The smell of the blood was overpowering. But most appalling were the three pairs of eyes that turned on him.

Farmer Wade held a large meat-axe and each son clutched at a dripping carving knife.

'Evening, Constable,' the farmer said. Suddenly his wooden face cracked into a smile. 'Come for your share, have you?'

'Have you a licence to slaughter and sell these animals?' Jack Lapham asked.

One of the sons stepped forward. 'Don't need one. These animals are casualties, see? Perhaps you'd like a nice steak – free of charge, of course.' The knife was twisting in his hand.

'That cow couldn't walk. We had to put her down,' the second son explained.

'And those two calves?' the Special Constable said, carefully keeping his eyes on those knives.

'Motherless,' Farmer Wade said. 'Poor things had to die.'

'That looks like a pig – don't tell me the cow was his mother too!'

'No . . . it was old – lame. Believe me, Constable!'

'I don't believe you. We'll just see if a jury at Winchester Court believes you, shall we?'

The man's hard face turned deep red. 'One more death won't make any difference,' he growled.

'Might as well be hanged for a cop as a pig,' his son agreed and stepped towards the policeman with the knife raised. 'Nobody will ever know what happened to you!'

Jack tried to force a calm smile. He didn't feel calm. 'Bill Anderson at the pub knows where I am.'

'You're bluffing,' the farmer's son said.

'Young man, London accent, greasy black hair. Came into The Grey Horse and tried to sell some meat. Your meat. That's why I came out here. If you know the young man I'm talking about then you'll know I'm telling the truth.'

'And if we don't?'

'Then I'm a dead man,' Jack Lapham shrugged.

For half a minute the only sound was the hissing of the oil lamps and the distant owls. Finally Farmer Wade ran his thumb along the edge of the meat axe and smiled. 'Only trying to make a living, Constable. Only trying to make a living!'

What happened next?

1 The Wade family killed the Constable and he ended up in the Farlington sausages.

2 Jack Lapham arrested the family. They went to court and were found guilty.

3 The Special Constable took a bribe. The Wades gave Jack Lapham meat and he kept quiet.

4 The Special Constable took a bribe. The Wades gave Jack Lapham meat but he reported them anyway.

> *Answer:* 2 The family claimed the animals were dead or dying so they were allowed to butcher them without a licence. However, the judge did not believe them. They were fined and imprisoned.

BUT there are many stories of less honest local policemen who took the bribe and kept quiet. Very often a whole village was involved. A pig was slaughtered and everyone got a joint – but the local constable had first choice.

Farmers had to tell the Government every time a piglet was born. But it was hard to keep a check. So, if a sow had 12 piglets then the farmer told them it was just 11!

One man was given a whole pig by his farmer-brother. It was hidden in the bath overnight. The man forgot to tell his sister that it was there. In the blackout she wandered into the bathroom. The candlelight revealed the pink, naked, bloodstained body in the bath. The woman ran out into the street screaming, 'Help! Murder! There's a body in the bath!' She woke all the neighbours and the man's guilty secret was out.

Ration fashion

If you couldn't get something during the War then you'd have to make do with something else. Women's stockings were hard to get – nylon for stockings was a fairly new invention and it was all used up to make parachutes for pilots. So, if you wanted lovely legs you would

● colour your legs

● draw a line down the back to make it look like a stocking seam

But, what would you use to stain your legs a brownish colour?

1 Gravy stock (like an Oxo cube)
2 Dye made from onion skins
3 Sun-tan lotion

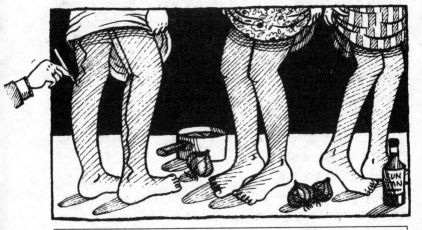

Answer: All of them were used by women at some time.

FAMOUS FIRSTS OF WARTIME

Lots of things were invented in wartime because they were needed to win the War. The Germans invented rocket missiles, for example. But which of the following were firsts between 1939 and 1945?

1 Dropping leaflets on an enemy town to give messages to the people (Messages like, 'Surrender now and we won't hurt you.')

2 Ball-point pens (for writing in an aeroplane)

3 Electronic computers (to calculate where a cannon shell would land)

4 Frozen food (because fresh food was hard to find)

5 Nylon (to make parachutes and nylon stockings)

6 Aeroplane ejection seats (so shot-down pilots could get out safely)

7 Radar (to warn you when enemy aircraft were coming)

8 Parachutes (to jump out of a fighter plane if you were hit)

9 Jeeps (to fight in rough countryside)

10 Women jockeys (because the men were fighting overseas)

Answers

1 No. This was done in 1806! Admiral Cochrane tied bundles of leaflets to the tails of kites. The messages were tied on with slow-burning fuses – when the fuse burnt down the leaflets dropped off. The kites were flown over the French coast. The method worked. (Perhaps you could fly messages over your house in this way. 'Have my tea ready, I'm nearly finished school!')

2 Yes. A Hungarian writer, Lasalo Biro, escaped from the Nazi invasion of his country in 1940 and took with him his idea for a ball-point pen. The British airmen were having trouble with doing navigation sums at high altitudes – fountain pens leaked and the ink wouldn't dry up there. In 1944 the British made 30,000 ball-point pens to help the war in the air. There are now more British ball-point pens than British people – and lots of people still call them Biros.

3 Yes. Mechanical computers had been invented by Charles Babbage in London between 1822 and 1871. But the first electronic one was made for the army in the United States. It began operating in 1946. It weighed 30 tons! That's 10,000 times as heavy as the computer this is being written on.

4 No. Clarence Birdseye was selling frozen food in 1930. But the first ready-cooked frozen food was made by the Birdseye company in 1939 – it was a type of chicken meal. (This gave rise to the horrible joke, 'Why did the one-eyed chicken cross the road?' Answer: 'To get to the Birdseye shop!')

5 Yes. Nylon was invented in New York (NY) and London (Lon) – hence the name, NY and Lon – Nylon! The Americans had used it for toothbrush bristles in 1938 and nylon stockings in 1940. But it wasn't made in Britain until 1941 – and the Government insisted it should be used to make parachutes, not stockings.

6 Yes. Invented by German aircraft designers in 1941. The first emergency ejection was in April 1941 when Major Schenk ejected from a test-flight and lived. The first British flier to try it was called Lynch. In 1946 he landed in the back yard of a pub . . . and was later found, safe (and happy) in the bar room!

7 No. Germany had working radar in 1934 and Britain shortly after. Both used it to detect air attacks – but neither side realised at first that the other side had it! (You get the name from what it did . . . RAdio Detection And Ranging.)

8 No. A man called Garnerin jumped from a balloon over Paris in 1797. He didn't have a hole in the top of the parachute so it gave him a very bumpy ride. This made him the first man to be air-sick . . . too bad if you were underneath!

9 Yes. The United States army wanted a vehicle that would be four-wheel drive and be 'general purpose' – or GP . . . or jeep. (GP – jeep, get it?) The first arrived in Britain in November 1941.

10 Yes. Judy Johnson rode Lone Gallant in April 1943. She was tenth of 11 riders, beaten by 30 lengths. (That wasn't too bad – the last time Lone Gallant had been ridden by a man he'd been beaten by 400 lengths!)

THE HOME FRONT

Soldiers fighting abroad faced dangers every day. They were sometimes a bit scornful of the Local Defence Volunteers. They called them 'Dad's Army' because they were largely made up of older men who were past being called up to fight in the British Army.

Still, these brave volunteers faced dangers of their own, stumbling around in blacked-out Britain, never knowing when they might face an enemy invasion! And would it come by sea or from paratroopers?

It was a hard life and a thankless job. Here are some examples from the Durham Home Guard Accident book. The entries may seem horribly hilarious – or they could be terribly tragic . . .

The dangers of Dad's Army

(There's no report on the injuries suffered by the marching men!)

17 August 1940
Volunteer J. E. Parker
Gunshot wounds in right arm and chest – accidentally shot by Volunteer Lumsden whilst on patrol
(Why worry about enemy paratroopers? Your own mates could shoot you!)

8 September 1940
Volunteer A. L. Mackay
Wounded in left knee. Accidental discharge of own rifle
(If the enemy didn't get you and your friends didn't get you then you could always get yourself!)

21 September 1940
Volunteer C. M. Blackmore
Gunshot wounds on left hand and right knee – accidentally shot by night-watchman at shipyard
(But if the night-watchman thought Mr Blackmore was an enemy commando, why didn't he kill him? Was he such a rotten shot that he only hit the poor bloke's hand and knee?)

And it wasn't just the fighting that was dangerous . . .
15 October 1940
Volunteer D. W. Skellern
Fractured ankle – collapse of table while attending a lecture in Durham
(Maybe it was a booby-trapped enemy table!)

Even the floor was out to get you . . .
19 March 1941
J. O. Davidson
Rifle went off and splinter from
wooden floor pierced thumb

So was your uniform . . .
29 May 1941
J. H. Cray
Sliced top of finger whilst fixing chin strap to steel helmet

And as for hostile dogs . . .
14 October 1941
R. Thatcher
On duty was knocked off cycle
by a dog – damaged knee
and wrist
(Perhaps it was a German Shepherd!)

The blackout was a problem too . . .
26 September 1940
Injured leg – run into from behind by a cyclist whilst
on patrol

And simply being old and unfit was a danger . . .
19 August 1940
Volunteer A. C. Moody
Died after practice at Whitburn rifle range. Inquest verdict:
death from heart failure brought on by the exertion on the
rifle range

Of course, the Home Guard would try to keep you fit.
All you had to do was survive the keep-fit sessions . . .

27 November 1940
Volunteer R. Simpson
Fell from vaulting horse – struck head. Died 30 November

And the War was not a job for men with false teeth . . .

28 June 1941
J. Oakenshaw
Tripped over gym mat, struck face against box – damaged mouth and broke false teeth

Of course, all these dangers meant you needed first-aid training. But a teacher's life is not a happy one . . .

21 September 1941
Volunteer J. T. Lowell
Severed tendon in back whilst giving first-aid demonstration

In fact a teacher's life could be rotten . . .
25 March 1942
Private E. Fowell
Instructing recruits on rifle range – received bullet wound in right thigh
(Would you shoot your teacher? Better not answer that one!)

But saddest of all were the innocent victims. The ones who had nothing to do with the War . . .
24 April 1943
Private Charles Stapler
Two broken toes – ran over a cat while riding a motorcycle
(There was no record of what happened to the cat.)

Home Front humour
The place where fighting happens is called the 'front' . . . so British soldiers were fighting on the **European Front**. But back home people believed they were in the middle of the War too. They described the people preparing for war here as being on the **Home Front**.

104

(**Note:** This joke was told in a theatre as part of a comedy show. The local magistrates were asked to ban it because it was too **rude** to be told on a Sunday!)

If you didn't have an indoor toilet then you'd keep a 'chamber pot' under your bed. The common name for a chamber pot was a jerry. A nickname for a German was also a Jerry. So a particularly bad joke of World War Two went like this . . .

Joining the Armed Forces was usually good for a laugh . . .

The Government encouraged a series of touring entertainments for people in factories and theatres. The organisation was known as ENSA – Entertainments National Service Association. They performed concerts and plays. Some were serious, some funny . . . and some dreadful. Unkind audiences said ENSA stood for *Every Night Something Awful!*

In fact, giving new nicknames to initials was popular in wartime Britain. The Local Defence Volunteers were called the LDV for short. Many people claimed that the LDVs were a bit cowardly and said LDV stood for *Look, Duck . . . and Vanish!*

ARP stood for Air Raid Precautions – religious groups sent leaflets to families and said the British people should ARP *Awake! Repent! Prepare!* (to die!)

106

The land girls

The women of Britain were encouraged to join the Women's Land Army – the WLA. Girls from the towns were asked to volunteer to work on the land. It was usually a hard life in primitive living conditions. Some were cold in the winter because they didn't have overcoats. And in summer they got so hot they often took their trousers off and worked without any!

The farmers weren't always grateful for the land girls' help. Sometimes the farmers and the girls got on one another's nerves. One girl was sacked. Her crime? She called the farmer 'pig face'!

Another land girl, Sylvia, had a choice between working in the dairy or working as a rat-catcher. She chose rat-catching – you had to milk the cows every day, but rat-catchers always got a day off. She passed her tests and started killing rabbits, moles, crows and mice as well as rats.

Four girls in North Wales probably held the record. In 14 months they killed . . .

- 7689 rats
- 1668 foxes
- 1901 moles
- 35,545 rabbits

Rabbits had a hard time of it. The Ministry of Agriculture said they were pests – and had to be killed. The Ministry of Food said they made a good meal!

So no one minded rabbit poachers any more. They sold the rabbits to villagers for one shilling and eight-pence (8p). If you skinned it and gave the farmer back the skin then he'd give you two-pence (1p) back – rabbit skins made good mittens!

It could have been worse – Adolf Hitler told the German people, *The lowest form of male is much, much higher than the noblest female.* So, girls, it's just as well he didn't win the War!

It could have been worse 3

Land girls had a hard life: the cold and damp caused several to suffer from arthritis at an early age. Still, it was generally a fairly healthy one. But women who chose to work in the armaments factories had a harder time. They had to make bullets, shells and high explosives. Many were killed or injured in explosions. The explosive mixture turned their skin and their hair yellow. They became known as 'Budgies'.

Oops!

Throughout the War governments and people made mistakes . . . some more serious than others.

- Bombing raids had stopped. The V1 flying bombs had ceased. On 7 September 1944 the Government announced that evacuation was ended. On 8 September 1944 the first V2 rocket fell on London and they were even deadlier than the V1s!

- In 1944 King Haakon of Norway was invited to speak on BBC radio. His speech was going to be 40 seconds too short so the radio producer sent to the record library for a fanfare of trumpets. The king finished speaking, the record was played – and there were music and screams and people shouting things like, 'Try your luck on the rifles, three shots a penny' and, 'Roll up! Roll up! See the bearded lady!' The producer groaned. 'What happened to the record of the fanfare?' 'Ah . . . sorry,' the assistant said. 'Thought you said funfair!'

- The British people feared the German airforce – the Luftwaffe. But the Luftwaffe lost the Battle of Britain. They also lost one or two other battles during World War Two. In February 1940, a Luftwaffe bomber sighted two warships and attacked them with cannons blazing and bombs raining down. Both ships suffered terrible damage. Unfortunately for the pilot, both ships belonged to the German navy!

109

- In May 1945, the war in Europe ended. To celebrate VE Day (Victory in Europe day) British warships in some ports fired their guns – it was meant to be a bit of harmless fun like November 5th bangers. A warship on the River Wear got it wrong - they used real shells instead of blanks. One shell landed on a Sunderland house two miles away. Two innocent people (who'd survived enemy bombing raids for six years) were killed!

THE ROYAL FAMILY

The Royal Family was particularly popular during the War. One reason was that they decided to stay in London to share the dangers of the ordinary people.

In fact Queen Elizabeth (the wife of George VI and the present Queen Mother) was pleased when Buckingham Palace was bombed. She said she was now just the same as the poor victims of the bombing in the East End of London . . . This wasn't quite true since she had one or two other comfortable homes to go to when the Palace was bombed. The East-enders often lost everything! But it certainly made the Royal Family more popular than they've ever been! Queen Elizabeth must have been the only person in Britain who was pleased to be bombed!

The King during the War was George VI. Did you know . . .

1 George first met Elizabeth Bowes-Lyon when he was ten and she was five. It's said that she gave him the cherry off the top of her cake!

2 George was never meant to be King. His older brother, Edward, became King. But Edward fell in love with an American woman who had been divorced. This was not on! Edward was given a choice – do you want the woman or the crown? Edward chose the woman, young George got the crown.

3 Actually, George was Albert. He used the name George as king because it was a regular royal name. But his friends and family always called him Bertie.

4 George hadn't been trained to be King. He wasn't very good at public speaking and had a stammer. His voice-trainer gave him tongue-twisters to practise on. Can you recite these? George could.
Let's go gathering healthy heather
With the gay brigade of grand dragoons
or
She sifted seven thick-stalked thistles
Through a strong thick sieve

5 When George was crowned in 1937 he had to take an oath. The bishops lost the place in the book at the last moment. The Archbishop of Canterbury held his own book for George to read from. But, George said later . . . *Horror of horrors, his thumb covered the words of the oath!*

6 One of the bishops then stood on George's robe and nearly brought the new king crashing to the floor. The coronation was the first time a king had been seen live on television. This was not a great event . . . there were just 2,100 sets working at that time!

7 When George and Elizabeth went on a royal visit to Paris in 1938 there was a lot of security cover for them. But, most peculiar, there were groups of stout Frenchmen leaning against some of the older trees on the route. The French were worried that the trees might fall on the royal couple!

8 The nearest the Queen came to being killed during the War was when she was attacked by a soldier . . . a British soldier! He had come home to find his family had been killed in an air raid. He deserted the army and made his way to the palace. The man found his way into Elizabeth's bedroom and she woke to find him gripping her ankles! The Queen didn't panic. She simply said, 'Tell me about it.' As he poured out his sad story she made her way to the bell and rang for help.

113

9 Britain sent its armies into Europe in June 1944. George VI wanted to go with the attacking armies. Prime Minister Winston Churchill wanted to go too. Churchill argued that if they both risked their lives and were both killed then Britain would lose its two leaders. In the end neither went!

10 Windsor Castle had a ready-made air-raid shelter for the Royal Family – the beetle-infested dungeons of the castle!

POTTY POEMS

The Second World War was a great time for music – everyone was singing to stay cheerful. The trouble was the words were pretty awful.

The *Blackout Stroll* was a cheerful dance . . . but it didn't take someone with half a dinosaur brain to come up with the chorus:

Everybody do the Blackout Stroll
Laugh and drive your cares right up the pole!

OLÉ!

Rotten rhymes

Could you have written a wartime song? Here are some classic lines – can you find the right words to complete them? Some are harder than others. The figures in brackets are the points you can score for a correct answer. Can you score ten without cheating?

1   **Run Rabbit Run**
    On the farm every Friday
    On the farm it's rabbit _ _ _   _ _ _
    (3)

2   **Roll Out the Barrel**
    Every time they hear that oom-pa-pa
    Everybody feels so _ _ _   _ _   _ _
    (5)

3   I'm Gonna Get Lit Up
You'll find me on the tiles,
You will find me wreathed in smiles
I'm going to get so lit up
I'll be visible for _ _ _ _ _
(1)

4   Knees Up Mother Brown
Joe brought his concertina, and Nobby
brought the _ _ _ _
And all the little nippers swung upon
the chandelier
(2)

5   Cleanin' My Rifle
Little bit lonesome, little bit blue,
Cleanin' my rifle, dreamin' of _ _ _
(1)

6   Bless Em All
Bless 'em all, Bless 'em all
The long and the _ _ _ _ _ and the tall
(2)

7   Lilli Marlene
I knew you were waiting in the street,
I heard your _ _ _ _
But could not meet
(2)

8 In the Quartermaster's Stores
There is beer, beer, beer you can't get near
In the stores, in the stores.
There is rum, rum for the General's _ _ _
In the quartermaster's stores
(2)

9 Let the People Sing
Let the people sing, sing like any thing,
Any sort of song they choose,
Let the people sing, let the _ _ _ _ _ _ ring
Anything to kill the blues
(101)

10 - - - - Me Goodnight Sergeant Major
_ _ _ _ me goodnight Sergeant Major,
Tuck me in my little wooden bed.
We all love you Sergeant Major,
When we hear you bawling 'Show a leg!'
Don't forget to wake me in the morning
And bring me round a nice hot cup of tea,
_ _ _ _ me goodnight Sergeant Major,
Sergeant Major be a mother to me!
(2)

Maybe the worst rhyme crime was in the song *Nursie! Nursie*, which came up with the awful rhyme . . .

> *Nursie! Nursie!*
> *I'm a-getting worsie.*

Yuck!

Vile verses

The Government tried to persuade people to eat certain types of food or do things to help the war effort by writing poems they could recite and get into their heads. Would you be persuaded to do what the Government wanted if you read these verses . . . ?

1 **Message:**

Poem:

> *The fishermen are saving lives*
> *By sweeping seas for mines.*
> *So, you'll not grumble, 'What, no fish?'*
> *When you have read these lines.*

(Instead you were offered whale-meat steaks – very oily and tough.)

2   Message:

Poem:

> *When fisher folk are brave enough*
> *To face the mines and foe for you*
> *You surely can be bold enough*
> *To try a kind of fish that's new.*

(Fish like ugly cat-fish that it spoiled your appetite just to look at.)

3   Message:

Poem:

> *If you've news of our munitions*
> ***KEEP IT DARK***
> *Ships or planes or troop positions*
> ***KEEP IT DARK***
> *Lives are lost through conversation*
> *Here's a tip for the duration*
> *When you've private information*
> ***KEEP IT DARK!***

4 Message:

WASTING FOOD IS
AGAINST THE LAW

Poem:

Auntie threw her rinds away.
To the lock-up she was taken.
There she is and there she'll stay
Till she learns to save her bacon.

The public struck back with verses of their own. The shortage of onions was mourned in one verse which ended . . .

My cupboard might as well be bare.
I sadly wander everywhere
And try to sniff the empty air
To scent a whiff of onion.

5 Message:

DON'T LISTEN TO BAD NEWS

STAY
CHEERFUL

Poem:

Do not believe the tale the milkman tells;
No troops have mutinied at Potters Bar.
Nor are there submarines at Tunbridge Wells.
The BBC will warn us when there are.

(A bit unlikely – a submarine arriving at Hastings on the south coast of England would have to travel 30 miles (48km) to Tunbridge Wells – over land!)

6   **Message:**

Poem:

R stands for rags, household Refuse and Rope.
And R stands for wise reclamation.
But remember that Rubber's more vital than most–
And please help the whole British nation.

R is for runs – and I modestly blush
R is for runs in your girdle.
May I suggest, if your corset's worn out,
It will help us to jump the last hurdle.

(This poem also had the curious line, *R is for victory!*)

7   Message:

Poem: (from an advert for wool)

There's more that goes to win a war
Than tanks and planes and guns!
Than men prepared to do their best
*To overthrow the Huns**

The Home Front too must play its part
And you can do YOUR bit
To help our gallant fighting lads
By starting now – to KNIT!

You cannot knit too many things
To keep out wet and cold;
Like mittens, helmets, socks and scarves
GO TO IT – young and old!

(Pity they couldn't knit a few tanks or the odd battleship!)

8   Message:

* Hun was a name
for a German
used by the British.

Poem:

Tittle tattle
Lost the battle

9   Children were also taught rhymes to help them remember important things. It was important not to talk to strangers. Not because they might harm you, but because they might be spies and you might let secrets slip. So you were warned . . .

If anyone stops me to ask the way,
All I must answer is 'I can't say.'

Mr Chad

During the War a new cartoon character appeared. A fat little face peering over a wall and saying, 'Wot, no ***?'. The face appeared everywhere, scrawled on walls and drawn in exercise books at school. Mr Chad would say, 'Wot, no wellies?' one day and 'Wot, no bananas?' the next.

Billy Brown

Posters appeared on London Transport for the most unpopular cartoon character of the War . . . Billy Brown. Billy was a chubby little man who was meant to remind you of how to behave . . . a bit like a teacher. The trouble was his advice made him sound very bossy . . . definitely like a teacher! Billy didn't get angry about waiting in a queue for a bus . . .

He never jostles in the queue,
But waits and takes his turn. Do you?

WARTIME WORDS

Every age has its own way of talking. If you lived in the 1600s then you might say, 'S'blood, sirrah, that kind-heart is a nimenog!' *I say, mate, that dentist is a fool!*

In the early 1900s you could have gone into school dinners and said, 'Great! Scaffold poles for dinner!' And what was on your plate? **Chips**, of course.

The Second World War brought its own slang. Can you match the slang to its meaning?

Spiffing slang

1	pit	a	smuggled goods
2	kerdumf	b	money
3	solid	c	a teacher who joins the army
4	akka	d	false teeth
5	niff-naff	e	mad
6	buckshee	f	face
7	pan	g	mouth
8	nutty	h	fuss
9	beertrap	i	free
10	sardine tin	j	crash
11	bolo	k	chocolate
12	schooly	l	stupid
13	rabbits	m	bed
14	railings	n	submarine

Scare your teacher:

(Don't panic but I just found a bomb in your desk! Hah!
I was just telling a big lie!)

Name that food

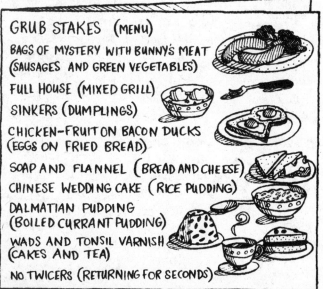

125

EPILOGUE

The Second World War was different from every war the British people had ever been in before. It wasn't just soldiers who faced injury and death every day in a strange country.

It was also the women, men, children and old people who stayed at home. Their courage was tested. So was their patience, their honesty, their determination and their sense of humour.

Most people passed the tests and amazed even themselves. Some didn't even bother taking the tests – and that surprised nobody. Those few used the War to make money and to make sure they came out all right.

And not everyone showed bravery under the threat of being bombed. An old man told this story which he swore was true . . .

A woman up at Tuppers Road heard the air-raid warning and panicked. She rushed out into the street wearing just a pair of stockings and a pair of shoes. An air-raid warden said, 'Aren't you going to put anything else on?' So she dashed back into the house and came out wearing a hat!

SNIGGER SNIGGER

'ERE'S YOUR 'ANDBAG MISSUS

OH, LORKS I KNEW I'D FORGOTTEN SOMETHING

She wasn't the only one to panic in the rush to a shelter. A young woman told this tale . . .

A woman came flying down Dean Road in her pyjamas. The buttons on the jacket were coming loose. While she was trying to do them up her trousers fell down!

The soldiers of Britain and her allies won the fighting. The people back home did their best to survive. And when the blitz was at its worst some even managed to raise a laugh or two.

In a small village in the south-west of England a German bomber swooped out of the sky, dropped a bomb and demolished the wall of a house. The woman who owned it rushed out into the road. As the plane roared off she shook her fist at it and yelled, 'You rotten beggar! We haven't even finished paying for that house yet!'

In the end, after six long years, Hitler's Nazi armies had been beaten. Britain and her allies had won on the battlefields, but nobody really won the War. The tens of millions who lost their lives were certainly the losers.

Many people still hate German people because the blitz in Britain killed so many. But as the War drew to a close, Britain blitzed the German cities too. We have to remember that the blitz on Britain cost the lives of an average of 50,000 a **year**. We also have to remember that a bombing raid by the Royal Air Force on the German city of Dresden killed 130,000 **in one night!** Not soldiers or weapon-makers or Nazis . . . ordinary men, women and children of Dresden along with countless refugees who were sleeping in the streets at the time.

Sometimes history can be truly horrible.

When Britain's blitz was at its worst the Britons were at their best. As Churchill said,

IF THE BRITISH EMPIRE LASTS FOR A THOUSAND YEARS, MEN WILL STILL SAY "THIS WAS THEIR FINEST HOUR"

He could well have been right.